W9-CLN-896

LUCKILY

VAN BROCK
FLORIDA POETRY SERIES

ANHINGA PRESS

2006

LUCKILY

POEMS

KELLE GROOM

VAN BROCK
FLORIDA POETRY SERIES
ANHINGA PRESS
2006

Cover art: *Zero*, 2003 (oil on panel) by Andrea Hersh
Author photo: Francis Miller
Cover design, book design, and production: C. L. Knight
Typesetting: Jill Ihasz
Type: titles set in Futura Light; text set in Minion

Library of Congress Cataloging-in-Publication Data
Luckily by Kelle Groom – First Edition
ISBN 0938078-87-9 (978-0938078-87-6)
Library of Congress Cataloging Card Number – 2006920072

This publication is sponsored in part by a grant
from the Florida Department of State,
Division of Cultural Affairs, and the Florida Arts Council.

Anhinga Press Inc. is a nonprofit corporation
dedicated wholly to the publication and appreciation
of fine poetry and other literary genres.

For personal orders, catalogs and information write to:
Anhinga Press
P.O. Box 10595
Tallahassee, Florida 32302
Web site: www.anhinga.org
E-mail: info@anhinga.org

Published in the United States
by Anhinga Press
Tallahassee, Florida
First Edition, 2006

for Michael Burkard

The Van Brock Florida Poetry Series

With this volume, the Florida Poetry Series
is dedicated to Van Brock, the founder of Anhinga Press.

CONTENTS

ACKNOWLEDGMENTS

I am grateful to the editors of the following publications in which these poems first appeared:

13th Moon: "Looking Right," "This Kindness"

Borderlands: Texas Poetry Review: "The Scrimshaw Artist," "Coat"

Clackamas Literary Review: "One Evening"

The Florida Review: "Handed They Went"

Folio: "Bird in Space"

Gulf Stream: "Half-moon"

Jack Magazine: "Take This Longing from My Tongue," "The Holy Dark was Moving Too," "Odeon in Noho"

Heliotrope: "Book of Lifesavers"

Lilies and Cannonballs Review: "Immortelle"

MiPoesias: "Lake Ivanhoe," "The Objects Everyone Dreams"

Pebble Lake Review: "Annunciation"

Perihelion: "Fire with Fire"

Pilgrimage: "Image of the Coat"

Poets Against the War: "What They Said"

Rhino: "Luckily"

Slow Trains: "Jack Kerouac's House"

Southern Gothic: "Ray Davies was My Bus Driver," "The Orange Bowl," "Recreating the Horse," "Lou Reed, the Reverend"

Swivel: "Mustache Rides For Free"

Unpleasant Event Schedule: "Why Did You Strike Him With Your Purse So Hard?"

In the poem, "Handed They Went," the italicized quote is from *Book IV, Paradise Lost* by John Milton. In "Pinkerton," the italicized quote is from *Mark 9:3*. In "Her Greenest Dress," the italicized quote is from Shakespeare's *Hamlet, Act 4, Scene 7*.

My gratitude to the Millay Colony for the Arts and the Atlantic Center for the Arts for support that provided invaluable writing time. I'm also grateful to the Edna St. Vincent Millay Society and to Elizabeth Barnett. Many thanks to Rick Campbell and Lynne Knight.

Dear thanks to Michael Burkard whose light shines on every page. My thanks to Terry Ann Thaxton, soul sister from the start, Andrea Hersh who painted across the hall and read typewritten drafts tacked to the barn wall at Millay, Terri Witek, Janean Williams, Bethany Bower and Noel Haynes, Ann Brady, Susan Hubbard, and Virginia Backaitis. All thanks and love to my family: Donna and Michael Groom, Cory and Diane Groom, John, Julie, Jessie, and Beth.

LUCKILY

I. BIRD IN SPACE

Tell me, what else should I have done?
Doesn't everything die at last, and too soon?
— Mary Oliver
"The Summer Day"

PINKERTON AND BUTTERFLY
GO TO THE DOLLAR MOVIE

In the morning, when I went to work, Pinkerton and Butterfly
were sitting on the front steps of the opera house, knee to knee,

doing a crossword puzzle. They looked up smiling, asked directions
to the dollar movie.

Because love can be like that, one minute you're at sea
and the next you're shoulder to shoulder reading newsprint

close as a slit throat, an obi — little package carried on your back,
little gift.

THE SCRIMSHAW ARTIST

In Oklahoma, there were days when he sewed
his chest to wire, like fish hooks in his skin,

and he hung himself from a tree, a mirror
that reflected everything.

In the store, he looked at the books on shelves,
said he wished he could read, dyslexic,

he'd never opened a book for pleasure, every word
work, and he looked at me with admiration

for this simple thing I could do, as if we weren't
separated, that when I read, he read,

the kindness in his face mirrored in my sleeps
and long winters, the way a few

wild flowers
became a thicket in his hands.

NIKKI FALLING BACKWARDS FROM THE MUSIC

In the spring, unable to swallow food anymore, with a hundred
mile an hour winds at her door, she put on her blue swimsuit,

walked down to the pool, took the steps slowly into the cool water,
swimming arm over arm, over and over, until she floats down

to the smooth stone, poured out like water, the soul in the body
like the tide under a moon, the gates open and close.

FIRE WITH FIRE

Kiki Smith said there aren't any memorials to burned witches
so she makes sculptures of women on pyres, arms outstretched,
using the same woman's body over and over,

a woman made of wax who is taller than Kiki,
and as she speaks, the wax woman appears to turn slightly
to listen, to look her in the eye.

What breaks my heart most about Joan of Arc is the examination
afterwards, before they raked her ashes,
luckily she was long gone: the crowd comes close to see her body

beneath her burned-off clothes, to know for certain if she was a boy
or girl, their looking makes my own chest cave as if I'm made of ash
myself or holding an invisible guitar

when I remember the medieval need to punish every cell
in a girl, forgetting that each palm is holy
no matter how you look at it

trying to destroy fire with fire,
it's what we do in Florida, when there's no rain
and wildfires in the woods, all the air trapped in a Bermuda High

balloon, the firemen burn brush in the direction a fire moves
to create an artificial clearing, the smaller fires burn out
the fuel, robbing the bigger, but if wind gusts and the fire

rages, nothing will contain it.

IMMORTELLE

The men sleep on deep blue mats, head to foot, in a metal tent,
windows open to keep them from panicking.

Weapons aren't allowed, but maintenance found dozens
of knives under the shed, clattering like silverware.

The children think the leaves of my green plant are flowers, a boy
carries a leaf high in the concrete yard, waving, girls taking

turns carrying the plastic pot, one girl asks if she is doing a good
job, balancing saucers and bells, trumpets, sweet everlasting.

COAT

A coat hung in a pine tree outside my bedroom window
like a seamless tan nightgown

displayed in the 1977 Kansas City exhibition
of North American Indian Art — the Algonquin coat or Cree

from the early nineteenth century, pre-reservation,
mooseskin coat with caribou, red and gray pain washed

away, the porcupine quills a woman chewed and softened
in her mouth, sewed on the shoulders, come loose.

I walked into the grass to get a closer look,
and a man in a blue truck stopped on the quiet dirt,

asked if I had seen a moose.
He'd found tracks up in the field

where the hunters park their campers.
No, but here is his thin coat, moving and alive,

waving as if on a clothesline,
waving like so many leaves.

JACK KEROUAC'S HOUSE

is down the street from my pink apartment,
past the Kool-Aid hibiscus and yellow trumpet
flowers that fall and melt like Barbie dresses
in the lake.

It's the corner of Clouser and Shady Lane,
single-story wood frame house
beneath a Florida Oak, and scarves of Spanish moss
the Seminoles used to wrap around their bodies
like bikinis.

Tin-roofed, back porch pad smaller
than a school bus aisle, unairconditioned —
A dozen cold baths a day sweating and dizzy.
A mouse hangs from a trap in the eaves.
The tub full of rust chips, tiny room, it seems
impossible he lived here with his mother,

Gabrielle — the tree the only spacious place,
the only shade as I walk outside,
and the Jack Kerouac Writer-in-Residence
ploughs into my car with hers,
the insurance buying me weeks of groceries,
and it's Jack Kerouac I thank.

BIRD IN SPACE

— *after Brancusi*

All the other cashiers ran into the stockroom
when the testy woman with the gauze
covered face came in, the square

of gauze growing bigger each week until
it couldn't cover the black in her cheek,
moving toward her nose like ants on the march,

black tattoo. She became nicer then, smiled,
said thank you, and one day told me
about a cave in a hot dry country

that she'd entered with her sister,
exposing themselves to an agent
that had first killed her sister

and was now chink chinking away at her.
I imagined something like the thick
yellow powder scattered around Egyptian

tombs, but didn't ask, just rang her groceries,
wanting to unhitch her copper bracelet, tiny
thorns jabbing every which way, little crown

around her wrist, face silting up, like a lake
filling with sediment, turning to marsh,
anatomy eliminated, revealing she'd gone.

DOORS IN THE GARDEN

The Operetta record player, drapes like long, ragged hair,
tear slits, flowers visible beneath the bronzy old.

Her green velvet reading dress with a little gold rope
across the breast like a stanchion

laid out on a divan, green and gold shoes beside it.
Liz doesn't show us the dresses folded in drawers to keep

the beads from dropping, or Edna's red hair glued on a doll,
or her tiny shoes where she'd left them.

She'd come here by way of Mabel Mercer, Liz and her husband
just back from Europe, broke in the city,

and a friend said Mabel was looking for a boarder to live
in her country house, so Liz went to the club and Mabel said yes.

She told this story in the drapey living room,
how Mabel would bring treats on the weekend, once she brought

a joint which made me laugh, thinking of their happy pot
smoking time, but then I realized Mabel was British,

maybe it was meat? Liz was reading Millay from the library
back then, and one day the librarian said, you know,

her sister lives down the road. Liz was intimidated, until one day
she told her husband and a friend to just get in the car, drove

the winding East Hill into Steepletop, just inside the stone stanchions,
but didn't dare drive up the curve, the three of them walking

to the house, and Liz's husband yelled out, *We are admirers*
of Edna St. Vincent Millay. Norma in the garden, stood up, came

toward them arms open wide, said Edna would have loved
you three, and brought them saltines and scotch down in the wet

bar, by the pool that is now a rectangle of slime,
and next thing you know, Liz and husband live in the guest house.

Before Norma died, she put Liz in charge.
The kitchen sink is a mess, but there's a big window

that *Better Homes and Gardens* installed for free in the 50s and a bird
feeder, an empty rope a bear pulled down.

In Edna's bedroom, I read the name
on the gold lipstick tube: Incarnate. A black purse

beside it, how little she carried. The library full of old
books, sun tanned spines, many of them signed, but we can't

open them. Liz likes that the barn I sleep in is a 1918
Sears & Roebuck model, likes how the blueprints show cows facing in

and cows facing out. She smiles and asks which way I face.
I wonder if the cows miss it, their stalls gone, their lives. A painting

on the living room wall shows Edna and Ugin swimming nude
in the pool in swoopy dolphin arcs — Liz hung it because she wanted

visitors to know they had fun.
A sweet photo in the room with two pianos — Edna smiling, young

she looks like Claire Danes. We walked up the stairs Edna fell down.
Outside, the fence is long gone. Rondelles on the doors in the garden,

removed, saved, they sound like a girl group, but they are like big
coasters with pictures of Edna and Ugin, for the wet bar, the pool, etc.

Andrea took my picture in front of one silvery door that we didn't
even try to open. Years before I'd stood in front of an Arthur Treacher's

yellow/blue door, around dawn, drunk, banging, begging to be let in.
I'd walked up the fake gangplank, the arc implying good times ahead,

confusing this fried seafood restaurant with the train car bar
where my boyfriend poured drinks — the last thing I remembered

was banging after hours on the bar's red metal door, like pure rust,
a hull. When I'd told Carrie at work, she said, *I live just down*

the street, I'd have taken you home. I imagined that kindness —
Carrie fixing me tea, her face always white like a cake, a calm

like the safety of my own bed, like Mabel Mercer, so maternal
Julius Monk said, *My dear, you are the equivalent of a breast-feeding.*

And now, at night when I miss you, when I knock from so far
away that I mistake a Wal-Mart bag in the dark of the rocking

chair for your hair, and reach for you, calling your name, plastic
in my hand, ready to walk over a thousand miles, eating bread

and cheese from a paper bag until I can knock on the wood of your
door, touch your face, when I miss you like that, I tell a story like this:

Ten years ago Paul was here, and a girl swam in the pool one night —
it was full of dead mice, slime of all kinds, but Paul said

she just had to swim it one time. Or, Edna wrote sheets of music,
and Liz would like to have a party and hear them all played.

Or, when Mary Oliver was eighteen, she drove here all the way
from Ohio, alone, knowing what mattered and driving right to it,

the Hidden Meadow, hills in the distance, blue and green
patient, gray far away, telling a story as much as singing it.

HANDED THEY WENT

All these I regret I never met — Reynaldo Arenas,
Kenneth Koch, Joseph Chaikin — it makes me want

to walk in the city with my hands held out
so that I might touch the hand of Nina

Cassian, and on the Henry Hudson all the light
in each window beside the river, each lamp

and curtain, all that time spent with the TV when
I could have been standing in a fire

escape looking for you, the people who jumped
holding hands, falling together,

handed they went, and eased the putting off
these troublesome disguises.

"SHE FOUND HERSELF ON THE WAY TO BYZANTIUM 1"

— after Joanna Jones

Dark blue floats like a robe on a sea-green sky, like scarves tied with
a circle of light — green-blue, as if you could wear the robe-scarves
and clothe your soul in folds of ocean. A little gauze coat with stars
on it, floats on the ocean in Marcel Duchamp's "Allégorie de Genre."
In the cave, Elijah cloaked his face and listened, the ocean of glittery
Milky Way stars as recognizable as a relative from childhood — one
dark cloud creating a hundred billion bright crosses with haloes,
calling, "This way, this way," like the silky circles around the faces
of icons and the domes under which they prayed. The Sombrero
Galaxy is farther out, with the Jewel Box, pink nebula like bubble
gum, blue Pleiades, the Horsehead Nebula, Keyhole, Hourglass,
Lagoon, the Cartwheel Galaxy, the Toby Jug, fox-fur, dust fingers,
silver river, heavenly seam, way of souls, and star-bright hat.

II. RAY DAVIES WAS MY BUS DRIVER

So I say Live,
and turn my shadow three times round,
  — Anne Sexton, "Live"

RAY DAVIES WAS MY BUS DRIVER

ray davies was my bus driver, and when the door slid open, i pushed
past his black coat to get off first, then apologized to his politeness,
the long bones

he asked for directions to charlie's oyster bar, and i pointed down
the sidewalk, walked into the arcade, empty, not one machine,
so i went to the bar, and saw ray leaving, head nodding, smile, i put
my chin down on a round table and wanted to sleep, but couldn't
get my wallet into my black zippered purse, olivia newton-john
trembled in the weak speakers, syruping my muscles

when a kid from school brought me homemade valentines in a manila
envelope, the outside pasted with hearts for other girls, carly
was one, but inside were five or six all swirling "k," scalloping, scissor-
cut mouths and petals, and i knew he'd have to stop this, this niceness,
his dark hair beautiful, sitting so close his khaki folds touched
my bareness between knee and thigh, he tried tucking my hair under
his green corduroy cap, it kept spilling

in the dark bar, my fingertips moved quietly under his clothes,
his body hiding my macrame, but if he didn't stop this, this love stare,
this open-handed adoration, my skin knew we'd have sex right
there in that chair

then he disappeared

and i sat across a two-top listening to a boy sweet as easter: the dinner
and basket, painted eggs, candy corn, too much chocolate, the bunny
bites always hollow inside, so you'd eat and eat, never satisfied

he said we can't do this anymore because i've been late to work
at the 7-11, three days in a row, they were docking my timecard

19

in ink, and because of jesus christ, i just nodded and smiled, i mean
this wasn't the same guy, and jesus would wish me bags of valentines

we left out the back where the cars parked in a forest, but i ended
up walking with acquaintance women who said i'd have to learn
to pump gas into the right car, and be on time for work

i skipped up the dark street, fast, away, and peggy lipton's ex-
husband side-swiped me, i actually had to push the fender away
from my waist, my feet, he swerved into the middle lane, and
almost hit a small comma traveling fast

he thought it was my fault, but apologized, gave me a ride
down a brilliant stone highway

THE ORANGE BOWL

luxury of a girl
on his chest
he held me down
over the stage
my curved back
his fingers drunk

morning my clothes
still jumbled in the eldorado
through the wet grass
and the trailer's icy
— it's meant for sting
in a few hours
(how is he not embarrassed
to have that name)

around my waist,
his work-tired arms
whiskey mouth
dreaming
the sheet
red again
where we'd locked
a necklace of dna
i was afraid we'd die
mechanical
setting the alarm

ONE EVENING

One evening I was late to a party and had to catch up —
    Kathy Zimmerman poured me a drink from seven bottles:

one evening I kissed my best friend's boyfriend, Brian Unger,
    and Kathy ran into the street screaming like an open field:

one evening I was pushed down on a dugout floor, scratchy-
    callused fingers hurting like insects, branches inside, until
    a bag boy drove up, shone his headlights on the ballfield,
    the coffins between seats:

one evening I peed at the golf course, in the tickling grass:

one evening I ran into the street to step in front of a car,
    but Burgess came after me, his arms around me
    like snow in the snow:

one morning I was too hungover to walk downstairs for a coke
    and ate grapes from a bowl and vomited into the bowl:

one evening I checked eight boys from town into my dorm,
    the desk worker frowning, one boy whispering don't ask
    my name, a closet full of bottles, Mad Dog beside my shoes —
    one boy missed his girlfriend, one took me to a movie,
    Halloween, a knife coming down in the woods:

one evening Ray took me to Mary's, Mary saying she's afraid
    of dying, and Janet leaned down and held her:

one evening a woman at Mary's said, when you called it rang
    here and pointed to the headset and phone:

one evening Donnie told me Mary had died after we'd gone:

one evening I had thirty days, and Joe K. gave me his yellow
    poker chip:

one evening a five-year-old girl touched my hand, asked
    how do you get your hands so soft?

one evening her dad told me she was twenty and drinking
    at school:

one evening her touch made me feel related, like a mother
    or a sister:

one evening Mike kissed my forehead:

one day he fell from a tree:

one day Jeff said you seem like someone I can talk to,
    then he was gone:

one evening we sat in an old church with a woman who spoke
    about the boat she burned her mother in, watching her
    go out to sea, and she spoke through the crying like you do.

HALF-MOON

A girl at the bar had a wire coming out of her finger with a tiny
cork at the tip — fingers bent toward earth, a V of black stitches
like a nest in her palm. Her throat cut clean on both sides — *it
didn't hurt, he'd sharpened the knife for three days.* She'd reached
up, blocked his hand, her finger breaking over her vocal
chords, past the knot of her hand he'd slit the other side too, ear
to ear, except the very middle. They'd been broken up three
months, she'd had a few beers, was sleeping when he'd broken
her window, crawled in, was only going to kill himself, but
since she was there, he sat on her chest, held her arms down,
talked for ten minutes drunk, then cut her arm to show he could
do it. When he left, she'd called 911 — *I don't know how. All I
could think was I want to be twenty-two.* Four doctors held her
head up while they sewed her neck shut. *When they took out
the staples I was scared my head would fall off. Could only lift it
up with my hands. One ear's numb for good.* The bartender
is sorry, buys us shots, kamikazis, little scryers like the green
light they shine on sun-deprived kids. When the girl stands
to leave, she's wobbly, and I'm nervous her head's not secure
at her bright scar, a half-moon.

LOU REED, THE REVEREND

wouldn't finish that bottle
of whiskey
with you

or stay
when you drew me
by the small of my back
against your chest
its cage of bone

where your heart
tilts
two clenched fists
drumming under skin

echoing that dark morning
in the catalina —
run on coffee, cigarettes
the ache in your heart
without sleep —
chaotic circus of early beats
upper chambers
quivering
before your heart stopped
cold

long seconds
before the cusps
of crescent moon
fired by a bundle of cells
flung open

and your heart
throbbed familiar
with the flap of valves
the turbulence of blood
chorusing

the dr.'s pills
red-line your eyes —
i try to teach
your rhythm
mine —
slow your heart's
erratic prayer

really, i listened
only minutes —
afraid of the racketing
the rests
of cleaving my breath
onto yours

wanted to drink
that bottle down
burn my mouth
with you,
spill like night
slick on pitch black
dirt — torn waves
of lou reed,
the reverend
skiff in, out
blood tide,
hurtling dark road.

A HOUSE LIKE THIS

I knew the girl from junior high.

Her husband on crack, backed the car out,
hit their baby in the driveway.
The baby lived, but she put the house up for sale,
filed for divorce, went skiing with the kids,
my boyfriend house-sat.

On the mantle was a photo of the girl, her long dark hair loose
like thousands of people talking at once.
One day, in seventh grade, she had planned to run away.
I wanted to give her my lunch money, help her
to get over the fence, light out.

She was standing up ahead with a few kids, a small circle
of miniature monoliths.
I spent the money on chocolate, but I remember her palm too
and her thanks — her voice separate from one high blend.

In my house, sometimes I heard people outside,
vomiting in my back yard, having run over from the bar
across the highway, yelling, pounding feet —
running back and forth across the highway.

In her house, she had huge boxes of zip-lock bags.
I left a wet glass on her wooden table — when my boyfriend saw
the cloudy circle, he acted as if I'd hit someone.
Closets full of dresses in dry cleaner bags — her bones smaller,
but I borrowed a handful.
When I wore them, I had to keep my arms close to my sides.

RECREATING THE HORSE

I say moon is horses in the tempered dark
because horse is the closest I can get to it.
            — Jack Gilbert, " Finding Something"

This proves that time is a circle, you say
handing me polaroids you've taken of yourself,
waist-length brown hair, flyaway
rooster cut sprouting from your crown,
face xanaxed, apostolic.

I've never known a man as afraid of the cold.
Dressing it like any wound, I tell you
I remember your body beneath mine. It helps
that your face is unchanged, dry kisses the brush
of a cricket.

I'm tired of the chain of bruises that fingers leave
on my wrist, climbing iron scaffolding at night
to lie down on stages, afraid of cancer bracelets,
losing the barefoot girl.
When I ask what you want, the third answer
is your true one.

FOR LUCK

I don't remember any talk,
the day that I left detox he arrived.
At home, my mother threw herself
against the kitchen wall,
little orange teapots crying,
I can't take her back.
On our side of the steel door
safe from harm,
we kissed, for luck, I guess;
I don't remember any talk,
falling together, his hair Jesus-long
and dark, some kind of wish
the kiss dissolved.
My four weeks up,
I walked outside,
wall between us
when there was no wall.

BLACK FEATHERS

I saw you fade from doorways, saw you broken loose on a train.
        Carrying brown bags overflowing with food,
I asked how you could have left with no goodbye.
        You were young as when I held the sad Italian girl
in your window, words from underwater gripping me
        as if I were slippery. I meant to see you off
at the airport, but when you let go, we were on a plane
        lifting off over water, my bags gone, purse, all money.
When we landed in Paris, my clothes disappeared.
        Leaving the airport, we walked down stone steps
into the city — you wore a long black coat like the angels,
        holding your left arm around my body, dressing
me, right hand below my heart. You said we'd see Rodin's
        knee, but we stopped at the house of your friends —
the son broke spaghetti into boiling water, the mother crazy
        and gray, alone on the fenced-in grass, her husband
just watched. The daughter gave me a sapphire dress,
        her grandmother's who she loved and missed,
soft cloth in a tissued box. You somewhere else
        in the house, but your hands still covered me.
I heard your voice, and said I was afraid of not finding my way
        back through the streets, the terminal, all that language
and water. Looking up from the sapphire blur, you were
        next to me on a train home, arms around my waist, hands
meeting at my hip, coat sleeves soft, black feathers.

PENNSYLVANIA

I found a roommate with a house made of yellow wood, two stories, a porch. He worked all night on roads, the job hours away. It was summer, our air conditioner broken — switched on, thin warmish air blew in a corner. He came home when it was light, always locking himself in his airless room with no fan and the windows shut tight. It must have been a hundred degrees. He hardly spoke. Sometimes mail came addressed to his last name, but with a Mrs. Thin, pale, with his blond hair tied in a rubber band, he carried a washing machine by himself. In a folder he read from, I could see a picture of a woman. When it's over I just want to look at him until he's gone. *I thought you might be homesick,* is what I would say.

THIS KINDNESS

Past the lake and the midges
incinerating in blue light,
into the laundry room —
key scarred dryers, screens
loose and rusty, a white-haired
woman folds warm quilts
into her shopping cart.
I plan to ignore her,
but immediately she smiles
and walks up close,
three white bristles on her chin,
and asks if I know what to do
if the lights go off.
I nod.

When she's shaken out her last
white quilt, I hold the peeling
screen door open wide
to the dock, the sulfurous
canal air, the old woman bumping
her cart past, smiling at this
kindness, she says, *Until tomorrow,*
see you then, her words
clinking like boat bells.

MUSTACHE RIDES FOR FREE

That's what his T-shirt said —
the black-haired guy
in detox with me —
I'd wondered at the open
invitation, its indiscrimination.

Janean said she'd never understood
what the phrase meant —
something to do with motorcyles and
handlebars — she asked about my first time.
I remembered the 4th floor study room
at Bridgewater, a dark-haired boy
from another school,
careless of the door's window
of anything but each other's mouths.

Before that
an angel dust dealer from Montana
with blue John Lennon glasses,
his apartment on the coast of Spain
pouring a licorice drink down my throat.

The dark-haired boy
before that,
from a family of dark-haired boys —
high school dealers with beautiful
motorcycles and lizard lazy eyes,
black pebbles that went nowhere.

The very first time —
10th grade party
a boy with glasses, blond
in a Nova

with his head
jammed against the glovebox
like a contortionist.

and earlier —
Lisa's older boyfriend
telling us
how someday we would love it,
and we yewed and pursed and pinched
our mouths, unbelievers.

DARK MOVIE

The day was long, my period started.
I went home from work, drank cold coffee in bed,
my pink cotton blanket soothed me, the four pillows, I slept.

A small animal caught my toe — a toe big as a small foot
and sliced it almost clear through, but the blood
and pressure fit the toe to the socket like two

large pieces of a broken ceramic vase can fit
if balanced, or a broken banana can be set in place,
squished a bit for stability. The doctor said to sew up

my right toe would sever my knowledge
of mathematics forever and advised against it.
I walked crying everywhere, wondering why

I don't say, "fix it," why I wait for someone
to take me back to the doctor, wait for infection
to set in at the neat, bloody ridges and lie on a couch

in a crowded room, eyes closed, sleepy, knowing you
would approach, my toe tingling, see me in this pathetic
state, but I couldn't straighten up, pull myself together.

I felt you touch my hair with your greeting, then you kept
going into the dark movie beyond my couch, as if unsurprised
by my surrendered loll, severed toe, tears, as if this were me.

ODEON IN NOHO

There's a beehive in the stars, and a coiled
party beehive wig with yarny, yellow bees
on the head of the beautiful girl who slipped
newspaper into the soles of her burned out
shoes. Janean wore a plastic dome sewed
to the front of her shirt, like a stomach-sized
version of a Trouble game, put a baby doll inside.
When the Greeks couldn't see the beehive
in the sky, there'd be rain and storms — wind up,
blowing lightning in a cloud across the bright lake.

III. LUCKILY

Sparks! It is possible

that in gazing at the moon
a time or two they became

the moon for just a moment.

— Michael Burkard, "Before the Dark"

LUCKILY

All summer I looked for white sandals, and there they were, fifteen
    minutes before the store closed, but the salesperson
    in the purple dress couldn't help.
A grandmother was beside her saying, *my baby's gone.* The mother
    looking for her in dresses, cosmetics.

The grandmother had shoes in her hands.
I held a sandal from my fingertips.
The salesperson phoned security, asked the grandmother
    for a description — she said, *I can't remember my baby's name.*

I understood how you can forget what's right in front of you —
    I'd had thirty years disappear at a sidewalk sale
    in this mall, tables of cheap shoes — and all of a sudden, every
    sound was cavernous, and when I'd picked up a platform shoe,
    I thought it was the 1970s.

It was like I fell into the shoe and couldn't find my way out.

Luckily, there had been a woman from school at the sidewalk sale
    who recognized my hypoglycemia; in the past, she'd
    alternated between sarcasm and kindness, but she let me lean
    on her that day, and I'd wound up sitting on a footstool
    in the health food store eating a protein bar on the house.

When the little girl appeared, her mother didn't raise her voice,
    she held her as if she was a glass girl, a petal girl, asked
    if she'd like these red shoes.

STEEPLETOP

The butterflies at Steepletop drank
from orange flowers like Gabriel breast-feeding,
one long pull, the body motionless;

then wings fluttering like hands clapping.
One landed on my breast, sky blue tank top,
as if I were a flower, drinkable.

At night, I walked to the Hidden Meadow and the old pool,
Edna St. Vincent Millay's locked-up house, with Shadow,
the caretaker's dog, half-blind with cataracts leading the way.

On the front porch, I peeked through a panel of glass, saw
Edna bigger than life — an oval portrait set on the couch.
I could see a bookcase inside, basket of sewing doodads,

stacks of books under a piano, old palette high and dry,
comfy chairs, a painting of a man on the wall.
Then, through the window, I saw a head inside the house

and started, but it was only me in a mirror,
reflection like the soul passing through hardness,
the material, not needing any key.

TAKE THIS LONGING FROM MY TONGUE

Two pages of *Caedmon's Song*
translated on a yellow legal pad,
white sheets, two white pillows,
(my blood permanent on one),

the scratchy polyester bedspread
with a big pin at the bottom,
the Green Goddess of the Eight Great
Obstructions, farmers from Peru

on a blanket nailed to the wall,
yellow oil that heats skin like hot
cinnamon candy, Red Hots burning
on your tongue, seven guitars —

it could still be freezing,
sharp folds of robe
dividing his panes of light.

PINKERTON

writes a love letter on blue paper
cries his blackberry voice
(you could lick his tears)
time brambling
cleft

oh lead us into a high mountain
into ourselves —
snow, so as no
fuller on earth can white

SKIN DECOY

I keep seeing myself on TV:
the Law School commercial in a courtroom,
a B & N in New York
waiting to ask Stanley Crouch
a question,
scooting over chairs to wait in line,
you don't measure life by sales,
my hair a bit darker, redder,
but that's just light,
me in a purple blouse,
smile for all, big eyes,
you do it because you do it,
it's a surprising, old lady voice — not me,
someone to the left — I swirl an Indian skirt,
that kind I hate —
rough cotton, string tie with little bells
on beads, a pooched-out waist,
you write because that's who you were,
I plagiarized "Love is a Many Splendored Thing"
on the piano in the basement when I was eight,
and thought it was my song.
Pete says get on TV, market yourself.
She wrote a little about her stroke,
she slurs a little,
she laughs, she isn't me,
a leaf chatters
on tar
like a person
walking by.

THE CARTOGRAPHER'S ASSISTANT

Temping for the bus company was like eating lunch
      at Chick-Fil-A under lights so bright in a booth so small,
you're practically falling into each other's pores,
      having to eat with your eyes closed. I had no sense
of direction even after seventh grade geography,
      my unsmiling, full-lipped teacher assigning me a partner
before we went outside to measure the sky,
      but I'd been deserted, left staring at concrete, a sharp edge,
and Frank Eidson, a boy in a blond corduroy jacket that matched
      his hair, took pity on my pink and yellow sunflower pants
and pointed, said a few words — compass points
      of kindness, nothing concrete. I never understood
arrows showing north in the sky, east in my right hand, west
      in my left. Map phobic, I got lost on every road.

In my eighth floor cubicle at the bus company were yellow
      wall-sized and computer maps — my job was to find rides
for people being kicked off welfare, get them to work or school.
      Each person was given 800 transportation dollars. I suggested
we buy them cars, but the blonde mapping woman said, *that's*
      interesting in a coffee philosophy way, and no one got a car,
people calling me to get to work at Trader Vics or McDonald's —
      no buses available, no carpool — they all took cabs,
almost $40 a day round-trip, no one even making that much
      in a day. How would they work when the money
was gone? I learned to find each person on the map — like looking
      for something I'd lost, scouring square inches.
There was a glass window around the entire floor, and some days
      I'd think of pitching myself through it to end
the air conditioned boredom. When they offered me full-time,
      I thought, just spin me around twice and ask me to point
north, I'll be free.

It was worse at Pilgrim Insurance, looking up 4,000 zip codes
         a day — no windows, no private cubicles, just
a tiny chair with a seat nearly the size of my butt. Then, I temped
         in a trailer for the developer who tore down the old
Navy base where I grew up. I could look out the portable window
         and see the excavated dirt that was the hospital
where my son was born — the office manager had saved bricks
         from the base but wouldn't give me one. I tried this job
twice, but couldn't remember which way to feed letterhead,
         the boss watching me —
and I cried as secretly as possible, but they brought in
         another temp who baked them brownies
and moved me behind a felt gray cubicle wall
         with a laptop and no work — facing a wall of carpet,
everything sideways. Before, I'd had a phone,
         a window, and Michael had called once,
said, *You sound like you're convalescing.* When I was tired,
         direction was the first to go.

LAKE IVANHOE

The leasing agent told him the building was gay Melrose,
but most of the neighbors ignored him, the way
they ignored each other,
and me, and the boy in love, until he smashed
not only his girlfriend's car, but every other car
in front of her apartment, a building's worth, including the police
car — broke every windshield — she didn't want to press
charges — he was so upset — but the neighbors insisted;

and the pretty girl who put a coffee table of magazines
in the hallway as if inviting you to read an article while you rang
her doorbell or walked up the stairs to your own apartment —
she played awfully empty music
       loud with her windows open,
smiling to that emptiness;
the fighting hallway girl screaming,
You're going to get me evicted,
and then she was gone; the family, then, just
the wife and baby, both so young, the hallway
smelling of purple bubble gum — white clogs
in the hall outside her door (bad feng shui), a tiny heart carved
out of each heel — her terrible screaming, the baby's
terrible crying, and I never offered to sit; the English

girl in the laundry room who, when I
complained about the trek down, said, *Yes,*
but it's nice to have so many washers — and do
all yr wash at once. Maybe
that's her secret for being happy
— finding something marvelous in
all your clothes tumbling — her husband
smiling the last time I opened the red door and saw
him, paying the pizza man — I wondered at his friendliness,

what good news had opened him, and then
the movers came and now I pass their empty
apartment, all the windows open, window to
window, people have lived here and gone for fifty
years, the moon a radium moon with three questions
almost: *What shines like that? As if it were living?*
Speaking in a silver tongue?

ANNUNCIATION

It was like meeting Madama Butterfly
backstage,
     but without that nervousness and
animation,

     like standing in the lattice
watching the day-old birds lift up their

heads, dark eyes, open their mouths wide,

then settle down against each other
                 for sleep,

the door
     that had been closed to him,
     and then the trees

in the yellow moon he made around,

reading my mouth, and all our clothing
     had about it the flowers they occasionally crush,
leafy trails which when embroidered, transform

the embroidery on the birds'
       wings in the nest,
       orange falling across

like Gabriel's when he leaned in to comfort you.

GREEN LAKES

A healer in Florida had told me about the three guardians.
Three spirits that look out for each person. Like Natassia Kinski
in the sequel to *Wings of Desire*, invisible angels in the library,
bending over readers unaware.

I was in the living room of a friend who had once brought me
flowers when I was in tears over love. She was a customer in the
health food store, and I was a cashier. Sometimes I took cooking
classes in her home. Her name was Harriet. We were friends
in a careful way.

Before Harriet died, I saw her in the magazine section of a bookstore,
but thought I would see her again, so hid in my nervous way, and she
went to Italy where, on leaving, she turned to thank her hosts and
then turned to walk down the staircase.

        Maybe she was giddy before she slipped on the stairs, caught
up in the thanking and goodbyes. She fell, hit her head, and died a
little later in an Italian hospital.

I thought of her husband, Paul, having to fly back over the ocean,
back to Florida, transatlantic, without her, an empty seat. Months
later, we were both in a coffee shop, and I tried to hide, but Paul sat
down with me, ate something sweet. Maybe all his guardians had
crowded into that one empty airplane seat to shine on him.

The sun was going down through the sliding glass on the healer and
me in the living room in Florida. I thought he would walk barefoot
on my back, but he said I was too weak. I shook most of the time.
There was a kind of low humming to my body.

He took my hand in his. It was time for dinner, and his wife
and Harriet and Paul were waiting in the foyer. They were going out,

were late, and someone sighed, jingled keys. This did not speed him up. His speed seemed to be the speed of the sun coming down.

I watched him the way I would watch the sun. As if the sun had dropped inside him, and he told me not to worry, ever. He said that I had three guardians, that everyone did. He didn't need to see his own guardians to know they were with him, but, he said, I could see if I wanted to.

⁊⧫

The reiki woman said your brow was wounded, and she helped you without touching. Afterwards, you had a short talk with her. She reminded you about your three guardians. You'd forgotten them. I'd forgotten them too.

In the coffee shop, in the car on the drive to Green Lakes, you asked who your guardians are. You said maybe they are Tom and Mary and your mom. It hadn't occurred to me that guardians came from life.

I'd been in the coffee shop, waiting for you to finish reiki, trying to draw a white flower. Dropping me off, you'd turned your head to say bye, and in the quickness I saw crying. Sky bleak, nine days.

At Green Lakes, you showed me the fairy tale path between the trees and the lake, glacial lake enchanting the trees, swirling the bark.

Fallen leaves star-red, orange, brown, floating on the water.

You and I left the muddy path, little puddles, and climbed a wooded hill to a green field, open.

I had to kiss you, a kiss in lake air, lake breath.

Walking out of the field, there is a bending path, and to the left, a little clearing, then woods. In the clearing was a deer. And another. And another.

It was as if each deer materialized, developed before our eyes, like a photograph,

like the orange painting we saw in Syracuse the night before, the third one — a faint woman sitting at a table in the green dark of a restaurant, some white marks to her right.

You saw other figures in the painting; they seemed to appear right before our eyes, a magic trick:
there, a man beside the woman in the green dark,
and minutes later, a girl in a bathing suit appeared to his right. Their bodies lifted, rose up from the restaurant's interior.

You said, *Look.* You said, *Another deer. Alone.* But all I see are leaves.

You're patient, saying, *No, look into the woods*, and I see more leaves, trees. I look very hard and cannot see.

Then you give me a landmark to look beneath, and there she is.

Oh. Looking right at us.

Patient too. Dark eyes. She could be made of leaves and air. Her look is of such tenderness. Like a tender mother. We stay with her a long time. After we turn to go, turn away from her, we look back. She has turned a half-circle to watch us go.

The Syracuse painter had said he liked chambers, and you had
written "secret" and smiled. The deer had risen up like that.

They had not moved as we moved toward them — we could
have been the sun they were watching before their white
tails danced into the woods. I had never seen deer remain
so near human company.

We walked toward the bending path, the edge of the clearing grass,
headed for the parking lot.
          And in front of us were three more deer. Watching us.

What do we do? I ask you, almost dancing. *We don't walk toward*
them, do we?

You say, *Yes.* The deer stay still. For this moment, my world
is the three deer and you. It seems that for the deer, we are theirs.
They stay even longer than the first trio — we could almost
speak conversationally.

Then the deer go around the bend, where one stays, waits for us —
          to deer we must be very slow —
I see his head above the turn in the bend, his deer face turned
toward us. Then he is gone, and we are in the bend.

BOOK OF LIFESAVERS

Why did I become a book of lifesavers when Karen became a TV?
Why did I need to lie flat on my pink bedspread, upended ship?
Why did my bed disappear when I became
a tiny library of candy, all of me falling back, folding in —
then, stretching out, accordianed?
When I was big, why did it feel like I'd fall off?
Do ghosts feel this spacious?
Do they have to restrain themselves from being erased,
fizzing like a galaxy of ginger ale?
Where would I have gone if I didn't pull back?

WHY DID YOU STRIKE HIM
WITH YOUR PURSE SO HARD?

Why did you marry him?
Why would a will be the test of your love?
You wound your arm up like a pitcher, and hit

the side of his face, his ear. After the airplane
fight, why didn't you go to him, sitting alone
in the back seat, kiss his cheek? He didn't want

to live in a trailer in Montana. You could have
said, *Big deal* or *Knock it off.* He plays invisible
cards in a happy and hopeful manner. Do you

moonlight to make enough? What do you hold?
Why were even the constellations upside down
or totally unfamiliar? I miss his silky petal skin,

and suede. Did you know he is not just a beautiful
curtain? The results of anger can be off by a factor
of ten. When you couldn't sleep, the night opened

her hands, made a bed for you in deep blue space
with stars. He isn't storage for phosphorus — the boy
who wants the job of feeding every cat in the world.

If someone dies in front of you in deep sand,
every time you see sand, you'll be afraid.
What is the necessity for cruelty? After a projectile

hits, things vanish and never a bone is found.
Tell me the best solution for mystery. His press
pouring in, his calm double for trees?

BATHING

I would unbutton his shirt
before I was crowded
with him in the shower,
the hours of damp on my neck,
long hair shrinking into tiny curls,
tight, childlike, in the mirror,
he said, *you don't always
have to look perfect*. I can't
tighten my stomach muscles
flat like his. The soap in his
hands to wash my body, hot
water soaking my hair, the soap
in my hands to wash his body.
Not to wash it away,
what can be washed away?
In the end, he said,
you're inside me, and went
to the Bahamas, Elushia,
where surfers leave food
in a cave for each other.

THE OBJECTS EVERYONE DREAMS

His hand and the towel on my mouth, the forgetting — like the old
Jewish story, how in the second before the sperm enters the egg,

the soul sees her whole life and chooses it, all of it. In a second of
the second, before the soul comes down, an angel slaps her

on the mouth, and she forgets everything she knows, everything
chosen: the memory pool, a wheel with the objects

everyone dreams. Mexico coming home with you to El Paso,
at fourteen, so lonely on the military base, desert and tumbleweeds —

the scratchiest hairdos angry and free-rolling in the backyard,
endless like the moon — one friend, Belinda, buying Skinny Dip

cologne, blue eyeshadow from the PX, but no photographs
not one, as if I wore an invisible cloak the whole time, aching

when I heard a motorcycle in the night, or sat in the right-hand
lane of an eighth-grade classroom, wearing a blue ring

from Mexico, I only crossed the border twice, but it's gone
or hidden like everything else right here with me all the time.

WHAT THEY SAID

The moon is back, silver cradle,
and they are saying ducks in a row,

something solid to stand on after.
They are leaving each other, and he's

on a ship at sea. The radio said
that the killed and wounded

watched from the grass.
The bookstore clerk rang up

my magazine — The Case Against
the War on the cover, and the clerk

said her son was a soldier,
she asked me to read the article

and tell her if it was okay for him
to be there. Six months later,

he came home for a visit and told
his mother he was in a special

military group, hand-picked.
The mother said he asked her,

What does it mean to be good at this?
Does it mean I'm good

at killing people?
For a long time the mother's

hair was white several inches
from the roots, then brown.

BIRDS

I was working a temp job in the dream. At lunch, I was served a blue
bird on a plate. An Asian girl sat next to me, her arm golden, her hand
moving a knife through her bird. I thought, if I eat mine, maybe I'll
have skin like hers, that shines. But I couldn't cut into the body with
the head intact, so the Asian girl popped the head off my bird as if it
were a Barbie doll. Two days later, I was sick with flu, wishing someone
would bring me soup. At the grocery, Stephanie waited on me — ten
years before we'd worked together in a health food store. When I'd
made her mad, she'd jump up and down — *like a little banty rooster,*
the old ladies said. But now she's always glad to see me,
tells me about the baby birds she buys, the newest one is gray, she's
up all night with feedings. She said she's a crazy bird lady now.

The Asian woman ahead of me was in a rush, almost left with no
receipt — I'd watched her watch the magazine rack, waiting for her
turn, blank. Stephanie said a friend complained that Steph hasn't
changed her nail polish in two weeks — she's too busy with the birds.
When I left, the Asian woman was coming back, passed me loudly
asking, *Where's my chicken?* and I knew Stephanie had made a
mistake, that I may have made her nervous. When I unpacked
the car, I saw an extra bag, but I had a fever, tired, I wasn't going back.
Inside I found her chicken: wings, three pieces. I'm vegetarian.

I haven't eaten fried chicken in twenty years. But I'd been living on
ginger ale and lime sherbet for days, so I decided to eat the chicken
— it felt like a gift, a dinner someone prepared for me, and it tasted
that way too, like the chicken my mother made for me as a kid —
Shake 'N Bake. I thanked the chicken and for a few minutes
tried not to think about the bones, the wing, to just eat, and let it
make me strong.

CLAUDIA GAVE ME BLUE TO PLAY

The beach kept emptying,
horseflies let me sleep.
A woman in a yellow bathing suit
and a man — fishing
in the ocean
when I woke up,
gone when I woke again.
When it rained
I wrapped my shoulders and chest
in a pink bath towel
hunched over
glad for it —
when I was fifteen I'd held
a pink towel to my breasts
in the bathroom mirror, thinking
one day I would have a dress
that color pink, and then I would be
beautiful, memorizing the shade
so I wouldn't pass it by —
I could see the clouds
passing over the blue,
patient for the sun I knew.

LOOKING RIGHT

When I interviewed for the grant research job at the hospital,
I was nervous and tried to remember what my lover said,
that I'm a plum, a natural.

I thought the interviewer would talk about grants or research
or fundraising in general, but her first subject was makeup.
I am allowed to wear foundation and powder, but it must be

natural and correspond to my skin coloring. Mascara is okay
if applied lightly; *true lip tones are acceptable.* Nail polish
may not be worn longer than four days without a fresh application.

My hair must be in an *easy-to-maintain style* and may be
confined by a *gold, silver, or tortoise shell barrette without
ornamentation. One small inconspicuous post earring per ear*

is allowed *(pearl, diamond, gold, or silver only)* as long as they
match, do not exceed a quarter inch, and are worn in the lower lobe.
I learned the hospital has its own gas station that accepts payment

in payroll deduction. On my birthday, I can receive 25 percent off
in the gift shop; however, I am only the first applicant, there are many
after me I'm told, and they may rerun the advertisement.

It will be a month before the job really starts, but if I am
the lucky applicant, in five years I will be fully vested.
I don't know what vested means, but in eight weeks I hope

to have made enough money to move to New York and never
see this hospital again. I don't even like *General Hospital.* On TV,
Heather Locklear was late for her interview, arrived in a tank top

(scoop neck, a hospital no-no), and was hired on-the-spot.
For this $13 an hour job I may wear only solid-colored suits
(no pastels), navy blue, hunter green, many shades of brown,

and oddly, purple is okay. My jacket may have *non-patterned buttons
in a color that matches the fabric.* The interviewer's blinkless eye
contact reminded me of an owl I saw in the park, staring at me

as if through two holes in a wooden fence. Hosiery is required.
Skirts must be *straight, A-line, or pleated* with hemlines no higher
than just above my knee and no longer than the bottom of my calf;

they must be *easy-care synthetic or a natural fiber that looks like
linen or fine wool.* The skirt may be fleck-patterned if, *from ten feet
away, it gives the appearance of an approved solid color.*

Bold plaids, lavender, pink, yellow, and mint green are banned.
A few departments allow female employees to wear pants,
but no knit fabric slacks. It was nearly 100 degrees outside,

my hair was wet and curling with humidity, forehead shining,
as I learned that turtlenecks are allowed, though no cap sleeves,
no sleeveless, no orange, rust, deep green or bright yellow.

I may not wear a shoe with a clear plastic heel or toe straps.
I am not allowed to have bad breath or other offensive
body odors. If I do not have my childhood immunization record,

I will receive shots for measles, rubella, tetanus, hepatitis B
and chicken pox. They will X-ray my chest. When I left,
the interviewer did not meet my eyes. In the rain, I lost

the parking garage, and by the time I found it, I had blisters
on both heels. I drove away so fast, I had to drive with just my feet,
my arms stuck in the navy blue suit jacket I was twisting off.

HELLO

Friday night sky bluish-purple-pink
and streetlights coming on —
the lake says, *you can kiss*
right here.
It says, *I see your yellow heart floating*
outside her pink apartment, I see your purple umbrella,
moondrops, gumdrops, the candy you're saving, necco wafers,
to slip from tongue to tongue, dissolving moon.
The lake says, ride with her in the little white car,
let her kiss you at all the stoplights, (Friday night date!).
Sometimes she feels the sea inside,
the clouds and sky, in the park the blonde girl
on her scooter stopped and smiled hello,
her whole face said hello, two gray cats
by the lake house came each in turn to lie on the sidewalk
so she could pet them, no pretending, and then you call
and she's out of breath to get to you, kissing you
in the just getting dark, her whole face hello.

HER GREENEST DRESS

Even after the stethoscope was invented,
people were afraid of being buried alive.
Whenever Hans Christian Anderson fell ill,

he'd put a note by his bed: *I only seem dead.*
He begged friends to cut his arteries before
they put him in the ground. (Terrified of death

by fire, he always carried rope.) I get claustrophobic
in an elevator, under a wave. Ophelia traveled
in a river *like a creature native unto that element*:

her greenest dress bearing her a while.
When Elizabeth was painted as Ophelia, she floated
in a cold tub's greenhouse light, caught pneumonia, died

and was buried with a handful of love poems (originals).
Seven years later, her lover dug her up for the manuscript,
exhumation famous for her perfect skin (laudenum) and long

red hair filling the coffin, a handful coming out like seaweed
with the poems. In Paris, 1785, skeletons were found in postures
of escape by workers clearing eight hundred years of bodies

from Le Cimétière des Innocents. The Code of the French
Empire had ruled no burials within 24 hours — feather, mirror,
and steam marking breath — but come an epidemic and the dead

were buried quickly, i.e., cholera in 1848 and '49, '66.
People wanted their hearts pierced, wrists cut, or a bell placed
at the coffin roof, attached by wire to the wrist; they wanted

food and water in easy reach, an axe. Before she died in 1880,
Sophie Elizabeth Wykeham asked her heirs to leave her coffin
open seven days; then, to cover it with glass and after waiting

fifty years, to bury her. But they got busy living, forgot
and new owners renovating, found her waiting just last year.
Because we want to say, *No. After a time.* Knock on the glass

and *let me out.* As if we might be found someday recovered
from a coma, a malaise. Miasma vanished! Holding our little
notes, exclaiming yellow Post-Its: (*I only seem dead*).

THE WALES HOTEL

In every picture, he had a slight cut above his nose.
and the boy spoke to me,
said he would find an adult to talk to, to get permission,
because he would be there all weekend, and we could play.

I kept turning around, reading the story, spinning almost
on the canopy from all the recognition.

Much later, I realized
that I had made a wish before I died.

You sent me a letter from the Wales Hotel,
and said that we would go there too.

I dreamed about the church in the pines,
you were trying to go there in the morning
so I tried, a crazy driver
on a winter road, and I wound up
inside the church, upstairs near where the beams
made a cathedral,

walking down stairs of wood
so soft each step felt like a slipper, sometimes moss,
and I carried a kind of stick in both hands, horizontal.
Downstairs, there was a tour, the boy's photographs
were on the wall.

HARMONY

It's different when you're not here —
for instance, there is always
too much food
and the waitress does not speak French.

C'est bon, avoir, oubliette the only words I remember.
Once I lived with a man who came back from Paris
and gave me poems in French about water — but he was angry
        at the grape juice
on his couch, a scratch on the mirror, dust — when I left,
he said, *stay.*

I am sitting at a table in a French café
in Florida —
earlier I sat in a French café in New York
with a man who criticized the smudges on my sunglasses,
the sand in my hair —
the table is the same size, a melody,
and the men at the next table converse:
Man One: *I got the gist, but are maps really what the logistics world
is worried about?*

Cows make me feel human because we're
so different — two voices that blend, two colors.
These trees — red with gray,
weird, off-key, palmetto vs. ocean line

or two people: letting a person have a bad time, the other
person making room, arms can hold you and
things that are sweet together.

STRANGER

The night I met her, she was shaking
hands, but when I came to her — she stopped,

looked into my face and smiled, put
her arms around me. When her husband

died a year ago, she wasn't doing
too bad until six months later. I said,

then it hit you. She was very old, and her
eyes were unfocused. I kept

trying to see inside because she'd
greeted me like someone known from

long ago. I think I may have sat in a
basement with her fifteen to twenty

years ago, and her husband was with us;
they made coffee and welcomed me, so that

the basement was cordial and light. I was shaking
then, but the light held me, like her arms,

as if she is the light herself, like her
husband is now.

THE HOLY DARK WAS MOVING TOO

The heat has gone to my head,
sun silt tapping,

a girl's sweater
whitening, porch

flames spinning
blue flight —

put on the dark
belt along the water's edge,
the trick is a fast burning solution —
grain alcohol burns itself up

before it has a chance to burn you
and there are no reflections
no objects to take hold of with your eye.

IMAGE OF THE COAT

The first few years of sobriety (when I went to at least daily meetings), light would just fall on me, and heaviness fall off — I could feel it and see it, like waking dreams. Once, walking across the mall parking lot, away from the health food store where I worked, looking for a quiet bench, I felt something heavy fall off, like a tire off a car. Another time, at the end of a meeting, during the prayer, holding someone's hand, I closed my eyes and saw and felt my hand in a room of light that felt like everything I'd ever wanted, and I imagined what it would be like if I could ever get my whole body into that room, and I thought it's the room of possibility — it was quick, just the moments of the prayer. I think I got to feel that way because I'd been so far down, that I was coming back to life. But while I was in Wellfleet I had another one in '99. I'd been there two weeks, in confusion, and went down to the harbor to walk. I walked by hundreds of small rocks piled together like a long bridge out into the harbor; then, just walking, and I felt a big coat had been taken off my shoulders — I hadn't felt the weight of it before, or the taking, just the lightness afterward, and the image of the coat.

SISTER GOLDENHAIR

1

Twigs in her hair
Bits of grass — waist-length wig slipping
Blue sky stings her eyes and the waitresses in the diner
Across from the Fort Pierce bus station
Won't let her sit at the counter
Drinking cup after cup of coffee.
Lonely for her I go back
Sit against the glass, its cold hinge

My hair a magnet too —
Leaves crackling when I've run my hands through.
Feathers baby's breath tiny spiders swinging.
She was on the ground last night
In wet grass and dirt — her wig's dusty falling
Asleep in a plastic chair with no rests for her arms.

2

When a drink was a plank,
I'd held a doorknob in my hand but the lock wouldn't turn
Hands like something mechanical — a thresher dragging me back.
Neighbors only a long jump away
But he suffocated me with his palm
Into blackness you can give up to

A slide into bright-light easy goodbye
Except for the sadness of the body empty.
I don't remember coming back —

Morning and highway and breathing again,
You make a space for yourself
Sing something quiet in your head,

Sister Goldenhair or the *Sylvia's mother said*
Refrain. Walking a waiting for the wave to end,
Migraine, broken bone
Labor that peaks and once it hits
It'll be easier in the desert
Measuring the circumference of the world.

Bus ticket guy says, *No* again — back to her plastic chair.
I've got four ones a couple quarters that might
Get her to St. Lucie,
Her eyes on a blur in the distance.
She scrapes my palm with her nails.
Walks to the ticket counter.

3

Damp concrete of the station
Makes me stiff.
Would turn toward the window
Feel the sun on my face
But the chairs are nailed down.
Stretch my legs over two seats,
Fold my arms on the back —
I can see her from the corner of my eye.

Since high school
Haven't sung out loud,
I know the words but not how to carry them.
She'd hear me across twenty feet of cement,

Make her smile.

Her bus arrives first. Through the glass she gets on,
Boys up front like soldiers out of uniform,
Young and healthy short hair confident
Laughing and laughing at the woman the twigs in her hair.
It rubs us like rags
Until we're completely still.
Covered with the marks of tools you don't recognize yourself
In classical figures mermaids reclining nudes —

Those ghosts of finish and marble sacrifice like fins for limbs.
The bus in the blue distance
A canvas with no window
Onto the wet field
The handle tried or the lung's hard push
Nothing but the road's quiet lines of desire.

Think of her stepping off at the beach —
St. Lucie or Jensen or Jupiter,
Sinking her feet in the sand,
Flinging off that awful wig.
Leaving it like seaweed.
Her hair damp underneath
Like a child's —
A breeze reaching her,
A kiss on a cigarette burn.

ABOUT THE AUTHOR

Kelle Groom's first collection of poems is *Underwater City* (University Press of Florida, 2004). Her poems have appeared in *Agni, Barrow Street, Crab Orchard Review, DoubleTake/Points of Entry, Florida Review, The New Yorker, Poetry, The Texas Observer, Witness, 88: A Journal of Contemporary American Poetry* and other magazines.

Her awards include the Norma Millay Ellis Fellowship from the Millay Colony, a Tennessee Williams scholarship from the Sewanee Writers Conference, and residency scholarships from the Atlantic Center for the Arts. She has also received grants from the Money for Women/Barbara Deming Memorial Fund, United Arts of Central Florida, and New Forms Florida. A native of Massachusetts, she lives in New Smyrna Beach, Florida.

THE VAN BROCK
FLORIDA POETRY SERIES